Leader Guide: Preschool

**Rainforest Adventure:
A Tree Top Bible Blast!**

by Sharry Hosfield

Augsburg Fortress 2008 Vacation Bible School Series

Bible Background Writer: Pamela Stalheim Lane
Editors: Lauren J. Wrightsman, Pamela Foster, Christy J. P. Barker, and Michelle L. N. Cook
Series Designer: Diana Running
Series Logo Designer: Diana Running
Series Image Artist: Gil-Jin Foster
Illustrator: Gil-Jin Foster

Scripture quotations are from the Contemporary English Version. Copyright © 1991, 1992, 1995 American Bible Society. Used by permission.

Created in cooperation with Our Sunday Visitor.

978-0-8066-6195-7

Manufactured in U.S.A.

1 2 3 4 5 6 7 8 9 0 1 2 3 4 5 6 7 8 9 0

WELCOME!

Reach new heights at Rainforest Adventure! During this Vacation Bible School (VBS), children celebrate being caretakers of God's creation through games, songs, stories, crafts, and more in a vivid rainforest environment. Throughout VBS, an emphasis on stewardship helps everyone learn that as caretakers of God's creation we share, give, grow, love, and praise.

As a Guide, you will lead a small group of kids through Rainforest Adventure. As you move together from the Opening Celebration to the activity sites to the Closing Celebration, you will have many opportunities to reinforce each day's theme and Bible story. As their leader, you will also have fun making friends and building relationships—the heart of VBS.

Ask your Rainforest Adventure VBS Director for a list of your small group participants, a schedule for each day, and the names of the activity site leaders and support staff who will be going on the adventure with you. This guide provides the support you need to be a successful Guide.

One way to integrate stewardship into your daily VBS activities is to find ways to talk about the Rainforest Adventure mission project, the Huch Uy Runa project (HUR). Huch Uy Runa is Quechua (an ancient Incan language still spoken by many in the Andean highlands) for "small important person." There are approximately 5,000 children living on the streets of Cusco, Peru. Rainforest Adventure VBS is working with *Huch Uy Runa*, (pronounced *who chi roo-na*), a non-governmental organization that since 1983 has taken kids ages 5-17 off the street, offered them food and shelter, and along with a lot of love and affection, has given them the opportunity to get an education and learn a trade. Offerings collected during your VBS will fund room and board, health services, and education for these kids. Remind children that any amount of offering will help the HUR, and offer genuine thanks for their donations!

Contents of This Guide

LEARNER RESOURCES

Your children may use some or all of the learner resources described below. Check with your Rainforest Adventure VBS director to learn which resources will be provided.

Preschool Bible Story Foldout

Children will need their Bible Story Foldouts each day during "Understory Bible Time," your Bible storytelling time. They can take these colorful foldouts home at the end of VBS and share the Rainforest Adventure stories with their families.

Tree Top Critters

Everyone on the Rainforest Adventure can learn about the daily themes and Bible stories with these fun and realistic looking Tree Top Critters!

- Shari the Butterfly (Day 1): This butterfly is very plain colored underneath. But on the tops of her wings she shares a beautiful blue color with all the world!

- Bill the Toucan (Day 2): Toucans give music to the rainforest with their loud and distinct cry. Further, all toucans are commonly known in many areas of the Neotropics as "Dios te de" (God gives to you) because the three syllable call of the Chestnut-Mandibled Toucan sounds like this expression.

- Tad the Frog (Day 3): The life cycle of the frog includes great changes and growth: from an egg, to a tadpole, to a frog!

- Esme the Macaw (Day 4): A pair of macaws raises one or two young each season in a tree cavity nest. The young birds often stay with their parents for up to two years. The adult parrots will not rear another clutch until the young leave the nest. As a result, the number of macaws increases slowly. The parents love their babies and take care of them because they learned love from their parents.

- Cleo the Monkey (Day 5): The howler monkey is the loudest monkey and the loudest land mammal. Their call can be heard for up to three miles! They praise God loudly and proudly!

Trading Cards

Each Trading Card features different images of the day's Tree Top Critter and the daily theme on the front. The back of each card features a Bible memory verse, links to online Web games, facts about the Tree Top Critter, and tips for fun family activities to try together. Each pack contains 20 cards, enough for four kids to have five cards each.

Pouch

Children wear their pouch each day to display their name tags. It's also a great place for storing their Tree Top Critters when they're not being used for an activity. There's also a place for their Trading Cards in the pouch. Collect the pouches at the end of each session. Be prepared with a few extras in case more kids join the group after VBS begins. Participants can take home the pouches and contents at the end of VBS.

DAILY SCHEDULE

A typical Rainforest Adventure day begins with everyone gathering together for the Opening Celebration led by your Rainforest Adventure Celebration Leader. During this time, children learn lively songs and explore the daily theme and Bible story through humorous skits and music. Check with your VBS director to determine if preschoolers will be attending the Opening Celebration. If they won't be attending, use the Free Play activities to help little ones get comfortable in the VBS environment. After the Opening Celebration, preschoolers and Guides gather in their learning space for all kinds of fun, active learning about the daily theme and Bible story. What follows is a suggested schedule. Use it as is, or tweak it to better meet the needs of your group of adventurers.

9:00-9:20	Opening Celebration or Free Play
9:20-9:40	Welcome to the Rainforest (Welcome Time and Rainforest Game)
9:40-10:00	Understory Bible Story Time (Bible story time)
10:00-10:20	Tree Top Activity Stations (Art Time)
10:20-10:40	Tree Top Activity Stations (Snack Time)
10:40-11:00	Tree Top Activity Stations (Helping Time)
11:00-11:20	Tree Top Activity Stations (Music Time)
11:20-11:40	Tree Top Activity Stations (Game Time)
11:45-12:00	Closing Celebration (or Sending Time)

RAINFOREST ADVENTURE PRESCHOOL STATIONS

Create different "Stations" in your learning space. Each VBS session will have options for six different activity stations each day—Bible Story, Art, Snack, Helping, Music, and Games. Create as many "Station" areas in your space as you have room for. Consider using the rainforest backdrops found in the Director Guide, and be sure to have supplies (instruments, art supplies, balls, books, toys, and so forth) related to each station on hand. Preschoolers will enjoy the variety of activities each day, and will thrive with a predictable daily routine. Have fun with these littlest learners!

*Allergy reminder: Before serving any food, check with parents and caregivers for children who have food allergies. Provide an alternative, if necessary.

A WORD ABOUT THE SKY HIGH STORYTELLING DVD . . .

Sky High Storytelling is an activity site that the kids from kindergarten through 6th grade may be visiting. If you are interested in having your group of preschoolers experience the fun Bible Story retellings on the DVD, please contact your VBS Director and ask about ways to involve your children at the Sky High Storytelling activity site. (Or see if you can borrow the DVD and play it in your space.)

Age-Level Info

Preschoolers (Ages 3–4)

God created each of us to be unique and special, and all of us have grown and developed in our own time and in our own way. Each of the children in your Rainforest Adventure group will be unique and special as well. One of the joys of your adventure will be to discover and delight in these differences. There are some things that may generally apply to most children in this age group. However, one of the things that you can count on is that you can never really count on this information applying to everyone!

Preschoolers need to expect that the adults around them will provide a safe and secure environment. Assure parents and their children that you have worked to prepare an appropriate space for your group. Ensure the safety of your space by making certain all equipment is in good working order and that the toys are age-appropriate and in good repair. Check for special food needs and other allergies. You may wish to encourage children to keep security items close by if they need them. Better to have a favorite toy or stuffed animal near than to have an unhappy child!

People of all ages learn in a variety of ways and it is in your best interest to provide a wide variety of learning experiences that appeal to all senses. At VBS, you will enjoy the sounds, sights, tastes, and smells of the rainforest with your children. Include both quiet and active play experiences as well as time for children to play together and opportunities for solo play. Notice and reinforce steps toward sharing and cooperation.

Young children are often working on either large muscle or small muscle development. Transition times are good times to get some wiggles out! Some activities will not take as long as expected and others will engage the children longer. Plan a few extra projects in case things do not go as planned. Try to let the children's needs dictate the time spent on each activity. It is not necessary to experience every activity. It is most important to have fun on the journey. Choose activities that seem most appropriate for your group. Relax! Have fun! Enjoy!

Supplies

Every Day

You will need the following supplies each day at VBS:

- Leader Guide: Preschool
- Preschool Bible Story Foldout
- Pencils
- Tree Top Critters
- Trading Cards
- Tree Top Tunes Song CD
- CD player
- Children's story Bible
- Adult Bible
- White copy paper
- Crayons
- Markers
- Adult scissors
- Masking tape
- Scotch tape
- Glue
- Stapler
- Hole punch
- Tissues
- Basic first-aid supplies

Additional Items

Each day there will be a few additional items needed for daily activities.

Rainforest Decorating Tips

Create a lush tropical area for reading stories or other quiet play. Bring in cushions or floor pillows to sit on. Towels or blankets will work as well. Rainforest stuffed animals or puppets will add to the environment.

- Set up the Rainforest Exploration area with books, puzzles, and games relating to the rainforest. The children will play here before class and during free play time. We will add appropriate items here each day.
- Put out a tarp and a small inflatable wading pool or small dishpans for water play. Have different water toys available each day.
- Plants! Plants! Plants! We need a lot of plants to create the rainforest atmosphere. Real plants as well as artificial ones will make the area look more like the rainforest. Mist or water the real plants every day to make it smell more like a jungle.
- Roll and crinkle brown craft paper to make vines to hang from doorways and the ceiling. Add large paper leaves to the vines to create a canopy overhead.
- Look online or in magazines for pictures of rainforest animals to hang in your space.
- Play sounds of the rainforest music or the Tree Top Tunes Song CD.
- Make a "Welcome to the Rainforest" sign shaped like a large tree to put outside your space. You can hang name tags here. Make sure to have each child's name on the sign.

WE SHARE

BIBLE BACKGROUND

Boaz Shares with Ruth

What factors shaped this story?

Naomi and her husband were Israelites who moved to Moab for economic reasons. While they were there, their sons married Moabite women, Ruth and Orpah. An illness killed Naomi's husband and her two sons. The custom was that if a man's brother died, then he would take care of his brother's wife as his own. But in Naomi's case, she had lost her husband and both of her sons. Her sons' widows, Ruth and Orpah, had no obligation to her or her to them. But Ruth chose to stay with her mother-in-law and traveled back to Israel with her. This was a remarkable and unusual decision. Foreigners, such as Ruth, were generally not valued and were considered outsiders.

At that time it was the custom (and the law according to Leviticus 19:9-10; 23:22) to allow the poor and widows to pick up the grain that the workers left behind and the grain at the end of the field. But Boaz went beyond the prescribed rules to provide for Ruth, inviting her to eat with the workers and drink their water and instructing the men to leave some grain for her.

What is this story about?

Boaz showed generosity to Ruth. He heard her story. He knew that she was a foreigner, but he also knew that she had been generous and faithful to her mother-in-law, Naomi, leaving her homeland to travel and care for her. Boaz also responded with generosity. Even though Ruth was a foreigner, an outsider, Boaz allowed her to gather grain in his fields, invited her to eat with him and his workers, extended his protection over her, and even instructed his workers to leave extra grain for her so that she could gather an abundance of grain.

Why is this story important?

Boaz was blessed with a great harvest. He responded to God's generosity by being generous himself—even to an outsider like Ruth. Likewise, we can respond to God's generosity by being generous with the gifts that God has given to us. We can share with others even if they are not part of our group or if their ethnic or social heritage is different from ours.

Bible Text

RUTH 2:1-17

Bible Memory Verse

Share every good thing you have.
Galatians 6:6

Goals

KNOW the story of Boaz, Ruth, and Naomi.

GROW to understand that God has given us much, and we are called by God to share what we have with others.

SHOW that we can be sharing and caring members of God's family.

READY FOR THE RAINFOREST

Transition Tips

- Flit and fly from place to place today, just like Shari the Butterfly.

- Transitions are difficult at this age. Patience and time are required to move children from one activity to the next.

- Make transitions learning experiences of their own. Try to make them fun, too!

Stewardship Sense

We live God's way when we . . .

- share God's love with others.

- share our toys with friends.

- share time with people who are lonely.

Rainforest Reflection

People share many things: feelings, food, laughter. This week you are sharing your gifts and talents with the children at VBS and you are about to embark on a journey with a group of children that will become a shared memory. Spend some time getting to know each of the children in your small group by name and say a prayer for each of them.

Kid Connection

Children in this age group are just beginning to develop the ability to share and are working on defining boundaries between what belongs to others and what belongs to them. Some may still think that they are the center of the universe! Today's Bible story introduces the concept of sharing. Encourage children to look for ways to share: have them color a picture together, glue a project together, or play with blocks as you begin your day together.

Preschool Prayer

Dear God, thank you for the things you have given us. We are so thankful for what we have. Help us to learn to share with each other. Amen.

Rainforest Term

Canopy: The top of the rainforest is called the canopy. The trees have so many leaves that they block the sun like a very big umbrella.

Mission Moment

If your VBS is participating in the Huch Uy Runa Project, use a map or globe to find where Cusco, Peru, is located. **In Cusco, there are many kids who are homeless and in need of help. This is what the Huch Uy Runa Project is about—helping children find a safe place off the street and in a safe place where they can live, receive medical care, learn, and love.** Talk with kids about ways they could share their time and earn extra money to give to the kids in Peru, such as helping a neighbor with yard work, helping clean the house, playing with or walking pets, and so on.

Preschool children may attend the Opening Celebration with all the VBS kids. Work with your VBS Director to find out if your group will be participating in this large group celebration!

WELCOME TO THE RAINFOREST

Free Play

Greet preschoolers and invite them to do one or more of these Free Play activities until everyone arrives and is feeling comfortable.

Rainforest Exploration Station

Bring in books, puzzles, games, puppets, and other toys relating to the rainforest for the children to play with and share.

Tissue Paper Butterfly

Make a copy of the butterfly on page 37 on card stock, one for each child. **Shari is a Blue Morpho butterfly. There are thousands of other kinds of butterflies in the rainforest. We will make our own butterflies. What color are you going to make your butterfly?** Glue the big pom pom for the head and the smaller ones at the ends of the antennae. Crumple up the squares of tissue paper and glue them to the butterfly.

Liana Vine

Liana vines grow all over the rainforest. They grow right up the trees to try to get to the sun. We are each going to make some liana vines to put our butterflies on. We will make other things to hang on our liana vine on other days. Take three strands of twine and tie them together at one end. Twist them until the twine begins to twist back on itself. Let it twist until it doubles all the way back on itself. Hang your liana vines up to decorate your room and add the butterflies.

Welcome Time: What Color Butterfly Are You?

Pass a beanbag or stuffed animal around to help children learn how to take turns. Have the children sit in a circle. **Welcome to the Rainforest Adventure. We are so happy you are here. We are going to go around our circle to introduce ourselves. When it is your turn, tell us your name and your favorite color of butterfly. I'll start. "My name is _______ and I like _______ butterflies."**

Rainforest Game: Fly Like a Butterfly

It can take a long time for a raindrop to reach the ground through all the trees and plants in the rainforest. When I throw the balloon up in the air, I want you to fly around like Shari the Butterfly until the balloon hits the ground. Then FREEZE! Throw the balloon up in the air and let it float down several times. Let the children take turns throwing the balloon. Invite other rainforest actions (walk like a monkey, chirp like a bird, etc.).

Free Play Supplies

- ☐ Books, puzzles, games, puppets, and other toys relating to the rainforest
- ☐ Card stock with butterfly outline (see page 37)
- ☐ 3/4" (2 cm) black pom poms
- ☐ 3/8" (1 cm) black pom poms
- ☐ Multiple colors of 1" (3 cm) squares of tissue paper
- ☐ 12" (30 cm) pieces of twine or yarn

Welcome Time Supplies

- ☐ Beanbag or small stuffed animal

Rainforest Game Supplies

- ☐ Non-latex balloon

UNDERSTORY BIBLE STORY TIME

Bible Story Supplies

- ☐ Costume—a plain-colored bathrobe or blouse and long skirt with an apron
- ☐ Cloth for a head covering
- ☐ A basket
- ☐ Some grain or a loaf of bread

Ruth and Naomi

Sing this story song to the tune of *"Frère Jacques."*

I will follow. I will follow.
Where you go. Where you go.
We will be together,
a family forever.
God helped Naomi.
God helped Ruth.

I will gather. I will gather.
Grain for food. Grain for food.
Baking bread together.
Sharing with each other.
God helped Naomi.
God helped Ruth.

Ruth loved Boaz. Ruth loved Boaz.
Boaz loved Ruth. Boaz loved Ruth.
All will be together,
a family forever.
God helped Boaz.
God helped Ruth.

We have a family.
We have a family.
God helps me. God helps you.
Share with each other.
Care for one another.
Thank you, God. Thank you, God.

Ruth's Story

Hello. My name is Ruth. I lived a long time ago, before Jesus was born. Let's all get comfy, and I'll tell you my story.

A long time ago I was living with my husband and his mom and dad. I was so sad when both my husband and his dad died. But I loved my mother-in-law and decided to stay with her. Women weren't allowed to earn money, so we had to rely on others to take care of us. I wanted to help take care of Naomi, my mother-in-law.

There was a kind farmer in the area who let us gather up the leftover grain from his fields. I would go to gather the grain that fell on the ground. Touch the ground. **Naomi would grind up the grain to make bread for us to eat.** Pretend to grind the grain. **Boaz, the farmer, had plenty of grain. He had enough for his family and for mine, too. He instructed his field workers to let me gather the grain every day. He told them to give me water to drink and to leave a little extra grain around so that we were sure to have enough.**

I gathered the grain every day. One day, Boaz talked to me. We became friends, and I came to love him. We got married and had a son. Naomi was very happy to have someone to take care of. She loved my son very much. God had watched over Naomi and me. God had given Boaz enough grain to share. God had given Boaz a kind heart. God had given me a happy life again. I thanked God for watching over me.

Bible Story Questions

Pass out the Preschool Bible Story Foldouts and display the story poster for today. Invite the children to look at the picture as you wonder together about the story.

I wonder . . .
    why Ruth decided to stay with Naomi.
    if Ruth was scared the first time Boaz came to talk to her.
    how happy she was when Boaz shared his food.

Story Review

Invite children to sing the story song found in the sidebar. Make up actions as you sing!

Treetop Activity Stations

Art Time: Wheat Painting

Today we are going to make a painting that looks like the wheat that Ruth collected from Boaz's fields. Wrap some rubber bands or string around an old block of wood. Spread a thin layer of paint on the paper plate. **Dip the block of wood into the paint like a rubber stamp. Stamp as many stems of wheat on your black paper as you wish. Use the cotton swab like another rubber stamp and dip it in the paint. When you stamp it on your paper, it will look like the seeds on the wheat.**

Snack Time: Shari-a-Little Snack Mix

Give each child a small cup with a different type of snack inside. Invite the children to pour their snack into the large bowl. Give everyone a chance to stir with the big spoon. Share small cups of the mixture with everyone.

Helping Time: Sharing Our Food

Let the children pack and repack food in a bag for the food shelf. Encourage the children to share food at home as well. Talk about people who sometimes need food shelves because they don't have enough to eat. Let them know that there could be children who are hungry in your community. **God gives us enough food, and we are to share so that no one will be hungry.**

Art Time Supplies

- ☐ Rubber bands or string
- ☐ Small block of wood
- ☐ Light colored paint
- ☐ Paper plate
- ☐ Black construction paper
- ☐ Cotton swabs
- ☐ Paint shirt
- ☐ Table coverings

Snack Time Supplies

- ☐ Small cups
- ☐ Several different types of cereal or small snack crackers
- ☐ Raisins
- ☐ Coconut
- ☐ Dried tropical fruit
- ☐ Large bowl
- ☐ Large spoon

Helping Time Supplies

- ☐ Grocery bags with handles
- ☐ Boxed, canned, and other appropriate kid friendly food for the food shelf

TREETOP ACTIVITY STATIONS

Music Time Supplies

- ☐ Parachute or large bedspread
- ☐ Tree Top Tunes Song CD
- ☐ CD player

Game Time Supplies

- ☐ 20 squares of paper with wheat drawn on them in each of the 3 colors to match the team color copied from page 37
- ☐ 3 small baskets each with a different color napkin or fabric to match the colors of the wheat squares

Sending Time Supplies

- ☐ Shari the Butterfly Tree Top Critters
- ☐ Trading Cards

Music Time: Wings on the Wind Music

Use the parachute while you listen to the Tree Top Tunes Song CD. Talk about Shari flying up to the top of the trees on the wind. **Feel the wind the parachute makes when we wave it. Wave it fast; wave it slow. Fling it way up high and lie down under it and feel it gently come down on top of you.** Encourage children to jump like a frog, wiggle like a snake, and other activities under the parachute.

Game Time: Glean and Gather

When Ruth gathered the grain for her mother-in-law, she had to separate the wheat from the stalk. We are going to do some sorting in this game. Scatter the wheat squares around on the ground and put three baskets in different corners of the area. Divide the children into three teams. Assign each team a color of wheat to collect in their basket. Have the children on each team collect the wheat that matches their color one at a time and put it in the matching basket. When all of the wheat has been gathered by the teams, they can sit down near their basket.

Sending Time: Share Like Shari

Have everyone sit in a circle. Pass out the Shari the Butterfly Tree Top Critters and Trading Cards. (**Child's name**), **you can share like Shari. God asks us to share.** Give each child a wheat square from the game you just played. **Let's pray together before we leave and think of some food that we can thank God for that is the same color as the paper wheat. Let's close by asking God to help us share like Shari the Butterfly. Every time we play with her, she will help us remember to share. I'll start the prayer. Dear God, thank you for spaghetti noodles.** Give children time to name other food they are thankful for. **Please help us share with others like Shari the Butterfly shares the beautiful colors of her wings. Help us to always remember to share. Amen.**

Rainforest Trivia

Shari shares her beauty with all the rainforest. When she needs to rest, she folds up her beautiful, blue wings and shows her wings' plain brown side to blend in with the rainforest.

Now it's time to attend the VBS Closing Celebration. If your preschool children won't be attending, close with the Preschool Prayer found on page 8. Remember to give the children any completed art projects and the day's trading cards to take home.

WE GIVE

BIBLE BACKGROUND

Elisha Gives Food to 100 People

What factors shaped this story?

In the previous stories in this chapter, we discovered that Elisha has done many miraculous things to help the people and that there was a famine in the land. In this story, a man brought food to the prophet. This was in keeping with the command to share the first fruits (or grains) of the harvest with God. The gift of 20 loaves of barley bread and the first grain of the harvest may have been a generous gift for the prophet Elisha, but it was a small amount for the number of people who had gathered around him. This miracle of the multiplication of food is one of a number of miracles that God performed through Elisha to care for God's people in times of need. It foreshadowed the multiplication of the loaves and fishes that Jesus did in the gospels (see Matthew 14:13-21; Mark 6:30-44; Luke 9:10-17; John 6:1-14).

What is this story about?

A man brought Elisha a gift of 20 loaves of barley bread and some of the new grain from the harvest. Seeing the food, Elisha commanded that the food be given to the people. The servant was skeptical that such a relatively small amount of food could feed 100 people. Yet Elisha was confident and proclaimed that God promised there would not only be enough, but there would be leftovers. Elisha then served the people and there was, indeed, food left over.

Why is this story important?

Giving to God and to others first is as much a challenge for us as it was in Elisha's day. In this story, we see how one man's faithfulness in bringing the first grains and the first bread from his harvest to God's prophet Elisha resulted in a great blessing for many people. One man's gift was multiplied by God to not only be enough but to provide a surplus for all the people. We, too, can give the first of our resources to God and to one another and be part of God's miraculous and abundant care for God's people.

Bible Text

2 KINGS 4:42-44

Bible Memory Verse

If we can give, we should be generous. Romans 12:8

KNOW the story of Elisha.

GROW in the understanding that all good things come from God.

SHOW love to others by giving of our time, our talents, and our belongings.

READY FOR THE RAINFOREST

- Have children who are line leaders for the day carry a gift box or bag as you move from site to site.

- Let the child who is speaking hold the gift bag for their turn.

- Put the daily characters in the gift bag to present to the children later.

We live God's way when we . . .

- give our offerings at church.

- bring food to a food shelf.

- send gifts and cards to people who are lonely.

Rainforest Reflection

From the day we were born God has given us gifts. Our very life is a gift, as are our family and friends. We are blessed at the Rainforest Adventure by the children, their families, and by the coworkers who surround us. Spend some time this day reflecting on the gifts you have received already this week.

Kid Connection

Children love to receive gifts. Gifts are tangible signs of love, and many moms and dads spare no effort to give children the things they need and want. Children of this age are starting to realize that giving gifts can be fun, too. In today's lesson we will be able to help them grow in their understanding of graciously giving and receiving gifts.

Preschool Prayer

Dear God, thank you for all the gifts you have given us. Help us to give whatever we can to help others. Amen.

Rainforest Term

Toucan: Bill is a toucan. He gives his music to the whole rainforest when he speaks and sings. He has a loud, beautiful voice!

Mission Moment

If your VBS is participating in the Huch Uy Runa Project, use a map or a globe to find Cusco, Peru, and have the kids guess how far it is from where they live. (Search the Internet for a site that would help to calculate the distance.)

What would you miss if you didn't have a home to live in? Talk with the children about the importance of having a safe place to live. **Think of how you might feel if you didn't have a place to live. Where would you go? What would you do? Do you think someone would give you what you need? Your donations to the Huch Uy Runa Project will give these kids what they need: a safe place for them to live, learn a skill for a job, and receive support and love.**

Preschool children may attend the Opening Celebration with all the VBS kids. Work with your VBS Director to find out if your group will be participating in this large group celebration!

WELCOME TO THE RAINFOREST

Free Play

Greet preschoolers and invite them to do one or more of these Free Play activities until everyone arrives and is feeling comfortable.

Rainforest Exploration Station

Add pretend or real rainforest food: bananas, oranges, coconuts, etc.

Giving Helpers

Set out hats, costumes, puzzles, puppets, and building toys that emphasize our community helpers. **Police officers, mail carriers, doctors, and teachers all give of themselves everyday at work. There are lots of people who care for us and who do things for others when they are at home, too. What are some ways we can be helpers and give to others?**

Rainforest Picnic

Set out toy dishes, a blanket, a picnic basket, and pretend food or real rainforest food. Let the children explore the picnic toys. **Elisha gave the people food when they were hungry. Pretend that we received food from Elisha and share our food like the farmer and Elisha shared their bread.**

Liana Leaves

Trace and cut out leaves for the liana vines from the leaf patterns on page 38. Make them out of different colors of green and different shapes and sizes. Be sure the stems are long enough to staple over the liana vine. We will make some other things to hang on our vines, too.

Welcome Time: We're Happy—We're Sad!

Distribute the happy and sad faces. **Right now I want to play the game "We're Happy—We're Sad." I will say something, and you hold up the face that matches what you feel.** Think of different "emotional" situations: a friend teases you, you receive a wonderful gift, your mom or dad makes your favorite food for breakfast, you lost your favorite toy, your puppy licks your face. **Let's think of other things that make us happy and sad together.**

Rainforest Game: Pin the Bill on Bill!

Use blindfolds if the children are comfortable using them. Otherwise invite them to shut their eyes tightly. Spin them around a little and give them a "bill" with double-sided tape on it. **Bill uses his beautiful bill to pull fruit and insects off of the trees to eat. Let's try to pin the bill on Bill.** Gently guide the child in the direction of the toucan that is taped to the wall.

Free Play Supplies

- ☐ Exploration Station items from yesterday
- ☐ Rainforest fruits or pretend food
- ☐ Hats, costumes, puzzles, puppets, and building toys with community helpers
- ☐ Toy dishes
- ☐ Blanket
- ☐ Picnic basket
- ☐ Different colors of green construction paper
- ☐ Leaf patterns on page 38

Welcome Time Supplies

- ☐ Paper circles with happy faces and sad faces, enough for each child to have a pair (you could use happy or sad face stickers, too)

Rainforest Game Supplies

- ☐ Blindfolds
- ☐ A large drawing of a toucan without a bill
- ☐ A "bill" for each child
- ☐ Double-sided tape

UNDERSTORY BIBLE STORY TIME

Bible Story Supplies

☐ Happy and sad faces from "Welcome Time"

God's Way Is the Way to Go!

Sing this story song to the tune of *"Hi Ho! Hi Ho! It's Off to Work We Go!"*

Hi Ho! Hi Ho!
God's way is the way to go.
We learn to share
to show we care.
Hi Ho! Hi Ho!

Hi Ho! Hi Ho!
God's way is the way to go.
Our voices raise
to sing God's praise.
Hi Ho! Hi Ho!

Hi Ho! Hi Ho!
God's way is the way to go.
We grow and grow.
There's lots to know.
Hi Ho! Hi Ho!

Hi Ho! Hi Ho!
God's way is the way to go.
We love to give.
That's how we live.
Hi Ho! Hi Ho!

We're Not Happy 'Cuz We're Hungry!

Let's bring out our happy and sad faces to the story area and get ready to listen.

Elisha had many friends. They were hungry. The ground was dry. The ground was hot. The ground did not grow enough food. **Hold up the face that reminds us of Elisha's friends.** Hold up a sad face.

One day, a man from another place brought some bread to Elisha. The man knew that he should give the first things that grew on his farm to God to say "Thank you." The man knew that Elisha was a man of God and he gave the bread to Elisha. The man was happy to give his bread to God. Let's hold up our happy faces. How did God feel when the man brought the bread to give away? Let's hold our happy faces really high because God was really happy! How did Elisha feel when he got bread for his hungry friends? HAPPY!

The man brought twenty small loaves of bread, but Elisha had 100 friends. There was not enough bread for everyone. Hold up the sad face to show how the friends felt. They were sad, weren't they? Elisha said to give the bread to the people. The man said there was not enough. Elisha knew that God promised there would be enough bread for everyone. God told Elisha there would be bread left over. The man gave the bread to the people. The bread was very good. And there was enough bread for everyone! There was bread left over, just like God had said. The people were very happy to have the bread. They were not hungry any more. Hold up the happy face. The man was happy that the people were fed and that his gift of bread had been a good gift. There was enough for everyone and there was some left over! Everyone was happy. God had taken care of the people. God takes care of us, too. God can use the gifts that we share to help other people. God is pleased when we give.

Bible Story Questions

Pass out the Preschool Bible Story Foldouts and display the story poster for today. Invite the children to look at the picture as you wonder together about the story.

I wonder . . .
  if Elisha was hungry, too.
  how God is able to provide for everyone.
  what I can give to help other people.

Story Review

Invite children to sing the story song found in the sidebar. Make up actions as you sing!

TREETOP ACTIVITY STATIONS

Art Time: Rain Sticks

Today we are going to make rain sticks. Color the tube with crayons or markers and decorate with colored masking tape and stickers. Leave about two inches (six centimeters) at each end undecorated. Place one wax paper circle over the end of the cardboard tube. Use a few rubber bands and glue to securely fasten the wax paper to the tube. Fold the small cardstock strips accordion style. You will need lots of folded strips. If you are using tin foil, loosely crumple it. Keep putting the folded and crumpled pieces into the tube until it is nearly full, then carefully pour the rice and seeds into the tube. Place the other wax paper circle over the top of the rain stick and fasten it securely with the rubber bands or tape. Turn the rain stick upside down to hear the sound of rain whenever you wish.

Snack Time: Bread for All

Use the cookie cutter to cut hearts out of the bread and use craft sticks to spread the jelly or cheese spread. **God gave food to Elisha's friends. God gives us food, too. Thank you, God, for food.**

Helping Time: Love Coupons

Think of ways children can give to others through actions instead of items. **We can show love by giving gifts. Gifts do not always have to be things. A gift can be something we do for someone else. We are going to make a coupon for someone in our family. Let's think of something that we can give that cannot go in a box, but is something nice we do for them. Maybe you want to give a hug, sing a happy song to cheer someone up, or you could help someone with their chores. We will write on the coupon what we want to give, and you can decorate the coupon with the stickers. When you give them the coupon, the person can ask you for the gift at any time.**

Art Time Supplies

- ☐ 12" (30 cm) paper towel or wrapping paper tubing
- ☐ Colored masking tape
- ☐ Stickers
- ☐ 5" (13 cm) circles cut out of wax paper
- ☐ Rubber bands
- ☐ Glue
- ☐ Several 1" (3 cm) strips of tin foil or cardstock
- ☐ 1/8 cup (240 ml) uncooked rice
- ☐ 2 Tbsp. (30 ml) seeds (popcorn, peas, or any sort will do)

Snack Time Supplies

- ☐ Two slices of bread for each child
- ☐ Grape jelly or cheese spread
- ☐ Craft sticks or plastic knives
- ☐ Heart-shaped cookie cutters

Helping Time Supplies

- ☐ Paper coupon on page 39
- ☐ Heart stickers to decorate coupon

TREETOP ACTIVITY STATIONS

Music Time Supplies

- ☐ Rain sticks made in "Art Time"
- ☐ Tree Top Tunes Song CD
- ☐ CD player

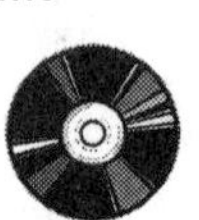

Game Time Supplies

- ☐ Beanbags
- ☐ Hula hoop (or circle created with masking tape on the floor)
- ☐ Bill the Toucan Tree Top Critters
- ☐ Trading Cards

Sending Time Supplies

- ☐ A large golf umbrella

Rainforest Trivia

Toucans are beautiful, friendly birds that live in hollowed-out trees. They fly in groups of three to twenty under the canopy of the rainforest. They use their big beaks to toss fruit to one another.

Music Time: Rain Music

Listen to the Tree Top Tunes Song CD and use your rain sticks to make music. **The rain that falls everyday in the rainforest is like music to the people and animals that live there.**

Game Time: Toucan Toss

When Bill the Toucan finds some food he grabs it in the front of his beak. Then he throws it way up in the air and catches it in his mouth. He is good at throwing and catching. If he misses, his food will go all the way down to the rainforest floor and he will be hungry. Let's pretend that the beanbags are Bill's food. We are going to try tossing the beanbags over our shoulder into the hula hoop (or circle taped on the floor). **Can we toss as well as Bill?** Have the children take turns throwing the beanbags over their shoulders. Have them try to hit the hula hoop or circle target. Give the children their Bill the Toucan Tree Top Critters and Trading Cards after they have taken their turns.

Sending Time: Raining Prayers

It can take ten minutes for rain to fall from the tops of the trees to the floor of the rainforest because there are so many leaves, branches, and vines in the way. We can pretend that the rain is falling on our umbrella. We will all stay dry. Let's say a prayer thanking God for the rain. Dear God, thank you so much for rain to make the grass green and the flowers grow. Amen.

Now it's time to attend the VBS Closing Celebration. If your preschool children won't be attending, close with the Preschool Prayer found on page 14. Remember to give the children any completed art projects and the day's trading cards to take home.

WE GROW

BIBLE BACKGROUND

Parable of the Mustard Seed

What factors shaped this story?

Parables are stories with a point, often using ordinary, understandable objects and situations to explain difficult ideas. Jesus often told parables to the people, especially when he talked about God's kingdom. The imagery of seeds would have been, and still is, accessible for all people. Yet Jesus' use of the mustard seed, a small, insignificant seed, would have been surprising. Often in Old Testament imagery, kingdoms were likened to mighty trees. In this parable, Jesus illustrated God's work is not just among the mighty, but is surprisingly active even in the smallest part of creation. This parable follows directly after the parable of the seed growing of itself (4:26-29) and is linked to the parable of the sower (4:2-9). In all of these parables, Jesus shows the miraculous and surprising work of God.

What is this story about?

Jesus said the kingdom of God is like a mustard seed planted in the ground. Even though it is a tiny seed, it grows into a large bush and protects others with its shade. Jesus commended its usefulness. The tiny seed becomes a bush with great branches, providing shelter and care for others.

Why is this story important?

The kingdom of God is not dependent upon the big and the powerful. While he could have chosen the mighty cedars or the tallest trees, Jesus chose a small mustard seed because he knew how fast and how well it could grow! Jesus knew the small mustard seed would grow and provide shade and shelter for birds as it was growing. Likewise, we start out small and some people may overlook us, but we can do many things pleasing to Jesus as we grow, too. When we are grown, we can work with those who are small and make a great deal of difference in sheltering and caring for them and their faith. The kingdom of God sees everyone's potential—now, tomorrow, and years down the road.

Bible Text

MARK 4:30-32

Bible Memory Verse

Grow and be happy in your faith.
Philippians 1:24

Goals

KNOW the story of the mustard seed.

GROW in the understanding that Jesus' love helps us grow.

SHOW love by sharing Jesus' story with others.

READY FOR THE RAINFOREST

- Moving in a fun way to get from place to place is a good energy burner and keeps children interested.

- Jump like a frog or swim like a tadpole.

- Think of other ways to get from here to there like rainforest animals.

We live God's way when we . . .

- read Bible stories to learn more about God.

- eat good food and take good care of our bodies.

- invite friends to VBS!

Rainforest Reflection

God could have created our world to be a static place where things stayed the same and nothing changed. Instead, our wonderful God made us so that we change and grow every day, not just when we are children, but as adults as well. Revel in the recent changes that you have enjoyed in your life and be grateful for an unchanging God in an ever-changing world.

Kid Connection

Growing is so exciting to a young child. Any kind of change is an adventure and every small accomplishment is cause for celebration. We are surprised and delighted when babies learn to walk and talk, even though almost all babies walk and talk at about the same age. We celebrate when a kindergartner loses a tooth—yet all baby teeth will eventually fall out. Your group of children is inviting you to share in their faith growth this week at the Rainforest Adventure. Celebrate and enjoy their growth—and you will grow, too!

Preschool Prayer

Dear God, thank you for helping us grow each day. Help us to grow to understand your love better. Amen.

Rainforest Term

Tadpole: A tadpole is a baby frog. In the rainforest, tadpoles grow up in tiny puddles that form in curled up leaves where rainwater collects. God provides a safe place for tadpoles to grow until they are ready to hop out!

Mission Moment

If your VBS is participating in the Huch Uy Runa Project, use a map or a globe to find Cusco, Peru. **How many miles is it from where we live? I wonder what the weather there is like today.** (Search the Internet for a site that would show you the weather there.)

Point out that growing doesn't only happen with their bodies, but with their faith and their minds when they go to church and participate in activities and celebrations. **The Huch Uy Runa Project allows the kids in Peru to not only grow in their bodies, but in their faith and minds as well, through classes they can take and by talking with the people who work with them. Your donations will really allow these kids to GROW!**

> Preschool children may attend the Opening Celebration with all the VBS kids. Work with your VBS Director to find out if your group will be participating in this large group celebration!

WELCOME TO THE RAINFOREST

Free Play

Greet preschoolers and invite them to do one or more of these Free Play activities until everyone arrives and is feeling comfortable.

Rainforest Exploration Station

Add children's story Bibles to the station today. **Jesus told lots of stories. The people liked to listen to Jesus tell stories because he made things easy for the people to understand.** Invite the children to look up favorite stories in the Bibles.

Babies Grow

Set out dolls, doll clothes, baby care items, and baby toys for the children to play with. Talk about things that babies can do and some things that babies are not able to do. Remind the children how much they have grown since they were babies.

Liana Flower

Set out many colors of tissue paper. Take three or four squares of different colors or choose all of the same color. Place them on top of each other and fold back and forth accordion style. Wrap a chenille craft stem or twist tie around the middle. Fluff apart the petals of your flower. Use the twist tie or craft stem to attach your flower to your liana vine.

Seed Study

Set out a variety of seeds and some magnifying glasses for the children to look at. Have them guess what each seed might grow up to be. Some seeds are easy to identify but some, like mustard seeds, are not.

Welcome Time: Babies and Big Guys

Spread out baby and adult animal pictures. **Let's see if we can match the baby animal to the adult animal. Some baby animals look just like their parents, only smaller. Some baby animals change a lot as they grow up. Tad looks very different when he is a frog, doesn't he?**

Rainforest Game: Tadpoles and Frogs

Have the children line up. Turn your back on them and call out, "Frog" or "Tadpole." Have the children either swim like tadpoles toward you and say, "Glub! Glub!" or jump like frogs and say, "Ribbet! Ribbet!" Let the first child to swim or jump to you be the one who calls out next time.

Free Play Supplies

- ☐ Exploration station items from this week
- ☐ Children's story Bibles
- ☐ Dolls and doll clothes
- ☐ Baby care items
- ☐ Baby toys
- ☐ 4" (10 cm) tissue paper squares in a variety of colors
- ☐ Twist ties or 6" (15 cm) chenille craft stems
- ☐ A variety of seeds
- ☐ Magnifying glasses

Welcome Time Supplies

- ☐ Magazine, Internet, or other pictures of baby animals and adult animals. Try to have adult and baby pictures of the rainforest animals that we are working with this week.

UNDERSTORY BIBLE STORY TIME

<table>
<tr><td>

This Is the Way!

Sing this story song to the tune of *"Here We Go 'Round the Mulberry Bush."*

This is the way
we share with friends,
share with friends,
share with friends.
This is the way
we share with friends,
Just like Jesus said.

This is the way
we love each other,
love each other,
love each other.
This is the way
we love each other,
Just like Jesus said.

This is the way
we go to church . . .
This is the way we pray to God . . .
This is the way
we read our Bibles . . .
Just like Jesus said.

</td></tr>
</table>

It Starts With a Seed

We are going to tell our story in a funny way today. I need all of us to sit close together in a circle with our legs crossed so we can reach each other's backs. Help the children circle up close together so that they can reach the back of the child in front of them. **We are going to draw today's story on each other's backs. Your finger will be the crayon and your friend's back will be the paper.**

Jesus told us this story. It started with a seed. (Draw a small dot on your partner's back. Don't poke too hard!) Put the seed in the little hole. (Draw a circle around the seed.) Pat the dirt around the seed. (Pat your partner's back.) Then came the rain. (Tap all of your fingers to make a rainstorm on your partner's back.) Out comes the sun. (Draw a circle.) Out pops the plant. (Draw a little plant.) Then some little leaves. (Draw some leaves.) Now some more sun. And some more rain. Maybe some wind. (Draw some lines across your partner's back). Doesn't that tickle? Finally, we draw a big, big tree.

Jesus tells us that the kingdom of God is like that tree. It started out small like the seed and keeps growing every day just like we do.

Bible Story Questions

Pass out the Preschool Bible Story Foldouts and display the story poster for today. Invite the children to look at the picture as you wonder together about the story.

I wonder . . .
>   how big is the biggest tree in the forest.
>   how long it takes a tree to grow.
>   how big I will grow to be.

Story Review

Invite children to sing the story song found in the sidebar. Make up actions as you sing!

TREETOP ACTIVITY STATIONS

Art Time: Froggy Fingerpuppet

Use the pattern on page 39 to trace and cut out two body pieces from the green felt for each child. Glue around the edges with tacky or fabric glue. Do not glue the bottom—that is where the finger will go. Use the pattern to cut out two arms for each puppet. Have the children glue the puppet's hands and eyes onto the puppet. Use the red felt to make a big smile. Use glue to attach it to the frog. With the children, make up a story using the puppet.

Snack Time: Tad Cookie

Use the craft sticks to spread the frosting on the cookie. Put two red cinnamon candies on for eyes and the red licorice piece for a mouth.

Helping Time: Faces of Faith

Jesus tells us about the kingdom of God. God tells us that the kingdom will grow a little at a time. Give each child some mustard seeds. Have the children draw a face on a piece of construction paper using glue. Sprinkle the mustard seeds on the face. **Jesus tells us that even faith as small as a mustard seed is important. We can tell others about Jesus even though we are still growing. Who will you tell about God?**

Art Time Supplies

- ☐ Pattern on page 39
- ☐ Pre-cut green felt pieces
- ☐ Felt scraps for arms
- ☐ Wiggle eyes
- ☐ Red felt scraps to make mouth
- ☐ Tacky or fabric glue

Snack Time Supplies

- ☐ Round cookie
- ☐ Green-tinted frosting
- ☐ 2 red cinnamon candies
- ☐ 2" (5 cm) piece of thin red licorice
- ☐ Craft sticks

Helping Time Supplies

- ☐ Mustard seeds
- ☐ Colored construction paper
- ☐ Glue

TREETOP ACTIVITY STATIONS

Music Time: Green, Green, Growing Machine

Have each child choose a motion with the streamer (*waving the streamer, touching toes with the streamer, putting the streamer behind their backs*). Have all the children stand close together. **We are going to make a green, green, growing machine. Take your streamer and do your motion while I play the CD.** Play the music and do your actions. Encourage the children to change actions if they wish.

Game Time: Grow a Little

Take off your shoes and enjoy the following finger play:

Put a little seed (pretend to take a seed in hand)
In a little hole (put the seed in a hole)
Pat a little dirt (stamp with your bare feet)
Pour a little water (pretend to pour with a hose or watering can)
Splash a little mud (pretend to splash with your feet)
Add a little sun (hands above head in a circle)
Pull a little weed (reach and pull a weed)
Grow a big, big tree! (reach up for the sky and stretch)

Sending Time: Barefoot Prayer

Gather the children in a prayer circle. Repeat the Bible Memory Verse. Hand out the day's Trading Card and Tad the Frog Tree Top Critter. As you hand Tad to each child, say, **(Child's name), you are growing every day in God's love.**

As long as we have our shoes off, let's say a barefoot prayer. Let's pray to thank God for one thing for each toe. I am going to pray for my family with my biggest toe. What else can we thank God for? Allow a short time for discussion and then pray, making sure to add the children's ideas.

Music Time Supplies

☐ One 12" (30 cm) green crepe paper streamer per child
☐ Tree Top Tunes Song CD
☐ CD Player

Sending Time Supplies

☐ Tad the Tree Frog Tree Top Critters
☐ Trading Cards

Rainforest Trivia

There are trees that grow above the canopy of the rainforest. They are called emergents. Some of these trees can be 250 feet (76 meters) above the rainforest floor!

Now it's time to attend the VBS Closing Celebration. If your preschool children won't be attending, close with the Preschool Prayer found on page 20. Remember to give the children any completed art projects and the day's trading cards to take home.

WE LOVE

BIBLE BACKGROUND

Jesus the Vine

What factors shaped this story?

Throughout the Gospel of John, Jesus makes "I AM" statements that reveal who Jesus is and that also identify Jesus as one with the "I AM" who spoke to Moses from the burning bush. In this final "I AM" statement, "I am the true vine," Jesus uses a familiar image. Vineyards were common in Jesus' day, and the vine was used as a symbol for Israel in the Old Testament. Jesus' disciples would have understood the comparison of the vine and the branches to discipleship. They would have been able to connect the gardener's need to prune the branches in order to produce more fruit with the stories of God's pruning the unhealthy vines in the Old Testament.

What is this story about?

Jesus used the metaphor of a grapevine to explain his relationship to his disciples. God the Father is the gardener. Jesus is the grapevine. His disciples (including us) are the branches that come out of the vine. The branches of a grapevine are dependent upon the main vine for their very life. If they are disconnected or torn off, they will die. They will be unable to bear fruit. Likewise, we as disciples are dependent upon Jesus for our life and for producing "fruit."

Jesus spoke about his relationship with the disciples. Because he loved them, he wanted them to know God's steadfast presence. He urged them to stay close to him and to embody his teachings. He reminded them that he chose them and calls them friends. He told them of his great love for them and even anticipated his coming death for them. He urged them to remain faithful, obedient, and steadfast, just as he is to God the Father. Finally, he commanded them to love one another.

What is this story about?

Jesus reminded his disciples of his great love for them and his steadfast presence with them. These statements apply not only to those disciples, but to all followers of Jesus Christ. Jesus tells them and us that he has loved us, has chosen us, and has commanded us to love one another as he has loved us.

Bible Text

JOHN 15:1-5, 7-17

Bible Memory Verse

We love because God first loved us. 1 John 4:19

Goals

KNOW the story of the vine in the Bible.

GROW to understand that Jesus tells us this story to help us understand God's love.

SHOW that we can share Jesus' love with others.

READY FOR THE RAINFOREST

Transition Tips

- Use a vine (green rope or yesterday's crepe paper) to travel with today. Have the children grab the vine as they walk together.

- Remind them that Jesus is the vine and that we are the branches.

- Give each child a stuffed animal (maybe animals that are from the rainforest) to care for today as they move from place to place.

Rainforest Reflection

Look online and at the library to find pictures of the rainforest. God created us to be caretakers of this beautiful world, and we show our love to God in the ways that we care for his creation, the earth. Research ways you can help care for the rainforest. Take some time to revel in the beauty of creation.

Kid Connection

Children thrive in loving relationships and never seem to get too much love and attention. They are also beginning to understand that sharing their love is important as well and they know they can show love in lots of ways. At the Rainforest Adventure, we will be teaching children that love comes from God. Because God loves us and we have been chosen to be God's special children, we have lots of love to give to others.

Preschool Prayer

Dear God, thank you for sending Jesus to teach us about your love. Amen.

Rainforest Term

Parrot: A macaw like Esme is one of the biggest of the 300 kinds of parrots in the rainforest. They use their strong beaks to crack seeds and shells of the fruits, seeds, leaves, and plants they eat.

Stewardship Sense

We live God's way when we . . .

- say, "I love you."

- hug someone we love.

- take care of our pets.

Mission Moment

If your VBS is participating in the Huch Uy Runa Project, use a map or a globe to find Cusco, Peru. Figure out how many miles it is from where you live. **What might the weather be like today? What language do they speak?** *(73 percent speak Spanish and 24 percent speak Quechua.)*

Most of the kids who live on the streets in Peru have been separated from their families and are on their own. What would you do without your family or their love? Talk with children about things their families do to show them that they love them. **People who work on the Huch Uy Runa Project are there to be a family to these kids, teach them, but most importantly, to show them that they are loved by God as well as by these wonderful teachers. Your donations will help these kids feel that they are loved.**

Preschool children may attend the Opening Celebration with all the VBS kids. Work with your VBS Director to find out if your group will be participating in this large group celebration!

WELCOME TO THE RAINFOREST

Free Play

Greet preschoolers and invite them to do one or more of these Free Play activities until everyone arrives and is feeling comfortable.

Rainforest Exploration Station

Add brightly colored feathers to the rainforest exploration station today.

Love Sticks Us Together

Set out magnets and metal items for the children to explore today. **Just as Esme the Macaw sticks with her babies because she loves them, the magnets stick together. We can't see the love that Esme has for her babies, and we cannot see what makes the magnets stick together either.**

Love Between Us Paper Friends

Use the pattern on page 40 to copy a row of paper dolls. **There is love between family members and friends just like the hearts between the paper dolls.** Color and cut out the paper dolls. Don't cut them apart!

Liana Leaf Rubbings

Put leaves on the table and cover with white copy paper. Use unwrapped crayons to color over the leaves. Cut them out and staple them to attach them to liana vines. There are so many different leaves in the rainforest so you will want to use many different shapes and colors for the leaves.

Welcome Time: Hearts Hold Us Together

We are going to pass this heart around. When it is your turn, tell us someone that you love. Then tell us how you show them that you love them. It could be something nice you say to them or maybe something you give them or do for them. Maybe you show them love by hugging them. I'll start. "I love _______. I show them I love them by _______."

Rainforest Game: Rainforest Relays

Create partner relays. For example, have the children hold hands and balance the beanbag on their joined hands. Have one partner crawl on all fours with the beanbag on her back. The other partner can go alongside to replace the beanbag if it falls. Make up rainforest relays of your own.

Free Play Supplies

- ☐ Exploration station items from this week
- ☐ Brightly colored feathers
- ☐ Magnets
- ☐ Metal surfaces, toy cars, cans, safety mirrors, etc.
- ☐ Paper dolls pattern on page 40
- ☐ White copy paper
- ☐ Dried leaves (place in a phone book for a few days to flatten)
- ☐ Unwrapped broken crayons

Welcome Time Supplies

- ☐ Small stuffed or paper heart

Rainforest Game Supplies

- ☐ Beanbags

UNDERSTORY BIBLE STORY TIME

Bible Story Supplies

- ☐ Surprise basket or bag
- ☐ Items that grow: seeds, plants, pictures of animals, babies, children, etc.

God's the Vine and We're the Branches

Sing this story song to the tune of *"She'll Be Coming 'Round the Mountain."*

God's the vine and we're the branches—Praise the Lord!
God's the vine and we're the branches—Praise the Lord!
God's the vine and we're the branches.
God's the vine and we're the branches.
God's the vine and we're the branches—Praise the Lord!

God will love and keep us always—Shout "Amen!"
God will love and keep us always—Shout "Amen!"
God will love and keep us always.
God will love and keep us always.
God will love and keep us always—Shout "Amen!"

Grow in Jesus' Love

Take your items out of your surprise bag one at a time to show the children. Ask the children to tell you what each item is and if they know what each thing will be when it grows up. **What does this plant need to help it grow? How will this animal change as it grows? Why do things grow?**

We talked about growing bigger and older yesterday. Today, we are talking about a different kind of growing. We are talking about growing closer to God.

Jesus told this story to his disciples. He told them he was like the vine and they were like the branches. He said the vine loves the branches and helps them to grow and he will love us and help us to grow. Jesus told his disciples that we were chosen by God and we will always be God's special children. Jesus loves us so he teaches us about God. Jesus said that we are his friends and tells us to stay close to him and he will help us grow. With Jesus' help, we will have what we need to love God and to love each other. Just like the vine gives the branches what they need, God will give us what we need.

Bible Story Questions

Pass out the Preschool Bible Story Foldouts and display the story poster for today. Invite the children to look at the picture as you wonder together about the story.

I wonder . . .
 how God loves everybody.
 how I can love everybody, too.
 if love can really help us grow.

Story Review

Invite children to sing the story song found in the sidebar. Make up actions as you sing!

TREETOP ACTIVITY STATIONS

Art Time: Paper Plate Esme

Staple two paper plates, one next to the other, to make one for the head and one for the body. Glue the wiggle eyes to the head and a triangle for the beak. Tape or glue the green feathers to the sides of Esme—or you could use green paper to make the wings. Use yellow triangles for her feet. Glue or staple a couple of tiny red feathers to the top of her head.

Snack Time: Stick Together Sandwich Snacks

Scoop a bit of frosting into each soufflé cup. Use craft sticks to spread the frosting on one vanilla wafer. Stick another on top. **Love is like the frosting—it sticks us together!**

Helping Time: Love Notes

Make a card for someone you love. Use any of the decorations to make your card. **A heart reminds us of love. Who do you love? Who will get your card?** Fold the paper in half. Use glue sticks, decorations, and stickers to decorate the card.

Art Time Supplies

- ☐ Small red paper plates, 2 for each child
- ☐ Large wiggle eyes or white circle dot stickers
- ☐ Yellow paper triangles for the beak and feet
- ☐ Very large green feathers or wings cut out of green paper
- ☐ Tiny red feathers

Snack Time Supplies

- ☐ Soufflé cups
- ☐ Frosting
- ☐ Craft sticks
- ☐ Vanilla wafers

Helping Time Supplies

- ☐ 1/2 sheets of construction paper
- ☐ Small scraps of paper
- ☐ Heart stickers
- ☐ Glue sticks
- ☐ Fabric scraps
- ☐ Anything else in the art supply cupboard that could decorate a fun love note

TREETOP ACTIVITY STATIONS

Rainforest Trivia

Esme loves her children very much, and they will live with her in her hole in the tree for a long time until they are ready to live on their own.

Music Time: 10 Little Parrots

Sing the following song together to the tune of *"Ten Little Indians."* Count on your fingers as you sing!

One little, two little, three little parrots,
Four little, five little, six little parrots,
Seven little, eight little, nine little parrots
Ten little parrots in the sky.

One little, two little, three little monkeys,
Four little, five little, six little monkeys,
Seven little, eight little, nine little monkeys
Ten little monkeys in the tree.

One little, two little, three little froggies,
Four little, five little, six little froggies,
Seven little, eight little, nine little froggies
Ten little froggies in the pond.

Make up verses of your own.

Game Time: Heart Hunt

Hide paper hearts all over the room before class (at least one for each child). **I have hidden hearts all over the room. Everyone look for them and, when you find one, put it in this basket.**

Sending Time: Heart to Heart

Have the children sit in a circle. One at a time have a child take a heart from the basket and give to another child. As they give the heart away, have them say to the other child, **"Jesus loves you everyday."** When everyone has a heart, pray together. **Dear Jesus, thank you for loving us so much! Help us to show our friends and families that we love them too. Amen.**

Game Time Supplies

☐ Small paper hearts
☐ Basket for the collected hearts

Sending Time Supplies

☐ Esme the Macaw Tree Top Critters
☐ Trading Cards

Now it's time to attend the VBS Closing Celebration. If your preschool children won't be attending, close with the Preschool Prayer found on page 26. Remember to give the children any completed art projects and the day's trading cards to take home.

WE PRAISE

BIBLE BACKGROUND

Jesus Enters Jerusalem

What factors shaped this story?

Jesus was headed toward Jerusalem throughout much of the gospel. It was a dangerous place for Jesus, being the location of both the temple and the occupying Roman government, since by this time both the temple authorities and the Romans were very suspicious of Jesus. Jesus and his disciples entered Jerusalem at the same time as many of the pilgrims who were coming to celebrate the Passover. The shouts of joy of the pilgrims were a combination of two pilgrimage psalms, Psalm 118:26a and Psalm 148:1. Although Mark, unlike Matthew, does not quote Zechariah, Jesus' entry on a donkey fulfills the prophecy that the Messiah would come on a donkey (Zechariah 9:9).

What is this story about?

Jesus was about to enter Jerusalem. But before he did, he sent two of the disciples ahead to find the colt of a donkey with the promise of its return. When the disciples brought it, Jesus entered Jerusalem, riding on the donkey. The people responded with praise and shouts of joy. They shout a word, *Hosanna*, that means both "Hooray!" and "Save us!" They honored Jesus and praised God by laying their coats in front of the donkey as Jesus processed to the temple.

What is this story about?

The pilgrims, singing and shouting praises to Jesus, were more right than they perhaps knew or understood. They were right to praise God for the Savior. They were right to call out *Hosanna!* They were right to say both "Hooray" and "Save us!" to Jesus. We worship and praise Jesus, because he is our Savior, the one worthy of worship and praise.

Bible Text

MARK 11:1-10

Bible Memory Verse

We will praise you and thank you, Lord. Psalm 35:18

Goals

KNOW the story of Palm Sunday.

GROW to understand that God sent Jesus to be our savior.

SHOW praise to God for all we have been given.

READY FOR THE RAINFOREST

Transition Tips

- Use music to get from place to place today.

- Sing, clap your hands, dance, hum, snap your fingers.

- March together like people in a parade. The line leader could even hold a baton.

Rainforest Reflection

Jesus rode into Jerusalem on a donkey in what is sometimes called the "triumphal entry." The people celebrated this new king in their midst. However, Jesus was unlike any king they had ever encountered. He came not to lord over them, but to be the Lord of heaven and earth. In what ways is Jesus different than you expected him to be? How has he surprised you? Thank God for the opportunity to teach these children about Jesus—the king of heaven and earth!

Kid Connection

Children in this age group may have attended a parade. Help them recreate the excitement that they felt and have them describe what they saw, heard, and smelled at the parade. Jesus had a parade because he was going to be king. Help the children begin to understand that Jesus is a different kind of king. He would not live in a castle or rule over one country. He would not have an earthly kingdom, but he rules over the whole world.

Preschool Prayer

Dear God, we praise you always as the king of heaven and earth. We love you forever. Amen.

Rainforest Term

Howler monkey: Cleo is a howler monkey. Howler monkeys live in the canopy of the rainforest and howl every night to let other howler monkeys know where they are. Their howls can be heard from miles away.

Stewardship Sense

We live God's way when we . . .

- sing songs that praise God.

- pray every day to thank God for all that we have been given.

- worship God wherever we are.

Mission Moment

If your VBS is participating in the Huch Uy Runa Project, use a map or a globe to find Cusco, Peru. **How many miles are we from Cusco? What's the weather like? They speak Spanish and Quechua. I wonder what kind of things they eat there?** *(Llama and Guinea Pig!)*

Many of the adults involved with the Huch Uy Runa Project don't ask for or receive praise for what they do. But they praise God for showing them how to help these kids in need. Talk with children about what it means to do something for someone without asking for recognition or praise. **When you donate to the Huch Uy Runa Project, this is almost the same, you are not asking for praise for your donations. But you can praise God, knowing that you, through these donations, will help kids in Peru who are in need.** Thank kids for their generosity and encourage them to pray for the kids in Cusco, Peru, even after VBS is over.

WELCOME TO THE RAINFOREST

Free Play

Greet preschoolers and invite them to do one or more of these Free Play activities until everyone arrives and is feeling comfortable.

Rainforest Exploration Station

Add rhythm and musical instruments today. Encourage the children to explore sound and rhythm with the instruments.

Praise Wavers

Make ribbon streamers by aligning lengths of ribbon and taping them together at one end. Wave them around to praise Jesus!

Liana Vine Monkey

Make a brown oval monkey body, a brown circle monkey head, and a tan circle for the monkey face. Glue all your monkey parts together. Add eyes, ears, nose, and mouth. Cut a spiral tail to hang the monkey from your liana vine.

Welcome Time: Praise Jesus!

The people waved palm branches when they saw Jesus coming and shouted, "Hosanna! Blessed is he!" Let's rip the paper to make some palm branches for our story today. We will wave our branches when we talk about our story later. What are some other ways we can praise Jesus? (*Singing, praying, loving others, clapping our hands, etc.*)

Rainforest Game: Through the Rainforest

Play the following game with the children, inviting them to flutter, fly, jump, peek, and swing through the rainforest as you call out the animals by name.

Fluttering through the rainforest, what do I see?
I see a butterfly peeking at me.

Flying through the rainforest, what do I see?
I see a toucan peeking at me.

Jumping through the rainforest, what do I see?
I see a tree frog peeking at me.

Peeking through the rainforest, what do I see?
I see a macaw peeking at me.

Swinging through the rainforest, what do I see?
I see a howler monkey peeking at me.

Free Play Supplies

- ☐ Exploration Station items from this week
- ☐ Rhythm and other musical instruments
- ☐ Lengths of different-colored ribbon (3–4 lengths per child)
- ☐ Strong masking tape
- ☐ Brown, tan and other colored construction paper

Welcome Time Supplies

- ☐ Green paper

Understory Bible Story Time

Bible Story Supplies

- ☐ Children's Bible time costumes
- ☐ Palm branches
- ☐ Praise wavers and musical instruments
- ☐ Donkey puppet or stuffed animal

Hosanna!

Sing this story sung to the tune of *"Did You Ever See a Lassie?"*

Jesus rides a donkey, a donkey,
a donkey.
Jesus rides a donkey.
Let's all praise the Lord!

The people waved palm branches,
palm branches, palm branches.
The people waved palm branches.
Let's all praise the Lord!

Shout and sing "Hosanna,
Hosanna, Hosanna!"
Shout and sing "Hosanna!"
Let's all praise the Lord!

Jesus Rides a Donkey

Help the children put on the simple costumes if they wish, and provide them with praise wavers and palm branches. Choose a few children to be Jesus and the disciples. The rest will be in the parade.

Jesus and some of his disciples walked toward Jerusalem for the festival. Have the children walk in place. **When they were almost there, Jesus said to two of his disciples, "Go over to that village. You will find a donkey tied up. Tell the owner that you need to borrow his donkey."** Have the two disciples go over to the donkey.

They went to the village and found the donkey and borrowed it just like Jesus had asked them. Have them bring the donkey back for Jesus to ride. **They put their coats on the donkey to make it more comfortable for Jesus to ride, and Jesus rode the donkey toward Jerusalem. Clip, clop, clip, clop.**

As Jesus and his disciples came closer to Jerusalem, many more people were walking along the road who put their coats on the ground to make the way smooth for Jesus. They shouted, "Hosanna! Praise to the Lord. Thanks be to God!" and waved palm branches. Have the parade children wave palm branches and their praise wavers. **Everyone shout "Hosanna!"**

Bible Story Questions

Pass out the Preschool Bible Story Foldouts and display the story poster for today. Invite the children to look at the picture as you wonder together about the story.

I wonder . . .
   why Jesus chose to ride on a donkey.
   what the disciples thought when they had to go borrow someone's donkey.
   how Jesus felt with all the people shouting, "Hosanna!"

Story Review

Invite children to sing the story song found in the sidebar. Make up actions as you sing!

TREETOP ACTIVITY STATIONS

Art Time: Praise Placemat

Spread some glue on a large piece of paper and place the tissue squares on the glue. Sprinkle the confetti on the glue and wait for it to dry. Cover your placemats with clear contact paper if you want them to last longer.

Snack Time: Rainforest Ambrosia

We are going to share a rainforest snack. All of these fruits grow in the rainforest. Put a taste of all the fruits in each child's bowl. Sprinkle with coconut if the children would like it. Or you could sprinkle your ambrosia with powered sugar and cinnamon, which also come from the rainforest.

Helping Time: Prayer Tent

We are going to make a prayer tent to help our families remember to pray at dinner. Fold the paper in half so that it will stand up. Write *We thank you, God* on each prayer tent. Glue pictures or attach stickers of things we thank God for on your prayer tents.

Art Time Supplies

- ☐ Large piece of construction paper
- ☐ 1" (3 cm) tissue squares of many colors
- ☐ Confetti
- ☐ Clear contact paper or laminating sheets

Snack Time Supplies

- ☐ Rainforest fruits could include: oranges, grapefruits, bananas, pineapples, mangoes, guavas, papayas, kiwi
- ☐ Coconut
- ☐ Cinnamon
- ☐ Powdered sugar
- ☐ Bowls
- ☐ Spoons

Helping Time Supplies

- ☐ Cardstock paper
- ☐ Stickers or magazine pictures of hearts, food, people, flowers, musical instruments, or other things we thank God for

TREETOP ACTIVITY STATIONS

Music Time Supplies

- ☐ Praise waver
- ☐ Tree Top Tunes Song CD
- ☐ CD player

Music Time: Praise Parade

Listen to the Tree Top Tunes Song CD and wave your praise wavers while singing. Walk around the area waving and singing. You may wish to take your praise parade outside.

Game Time: Jesus Has Come At Last

Do the following action rhyme. Start with one child by you and the others on the other side of the road.

There was one *(two, three . . .)* **little child(ren) by the side of the road**
Who was *(were)* **waiting for Jesus to pass.**
He/she *(They)* **was** *(were)* **waving his/her** *(their)* **palm branch(es) over his/her** *(their)* **head(s).**
For Jesus has come at last.

Continue adding children one at a time until everyone in the class is waving their palm branches. Say the following when everyone is on the same side of the road.

There was a large crowd by the side of the road
Waiting for Jesus to pass.
They were waving palm branches over their heads
For Jesus had come at last. "Hosanna! Hosanna! HOSANNA!"

Encourage the children to yell, "Hosanna!" with you.

Rainforest Trivia

When a group of howler monkeys come to a break in the trees, the grown-up monkeys hold each other's hands and tails so the little monkeys can scamper across the big monkeys' back bridge.

Sending Time: We Praise You God!

Gather for a prayer time. Wave the palm branches after every petition of the prayer.

Dear God, we praise you! (Wave)
You have taught us to share. (Wave)
You have taught us to give. (Wave)
You help us grow! (Wave)
We praise you! (Wave)
Amen.

Hand out the Cleo the Monkey Tree Top Critter and Trading Cards to each child. **(*Child's name*), you can praise God like Cleo.**

Sending Time Supplies

- ☐ Palm branches from "Welcome Time"
- ☐ Cleo the Monkey Tree Top Critters
- ☐ Trading Cards

Now it's time to attend the VBS Closing Celebration. If your preschool children won't be attending, close with the Preschool Prayer found on page 32. Remember to give the children any completed art projects and the day's trading cards to take home.

Love Coupon

This coupon entitles the holder to

receive one _______________________.

Love,

____

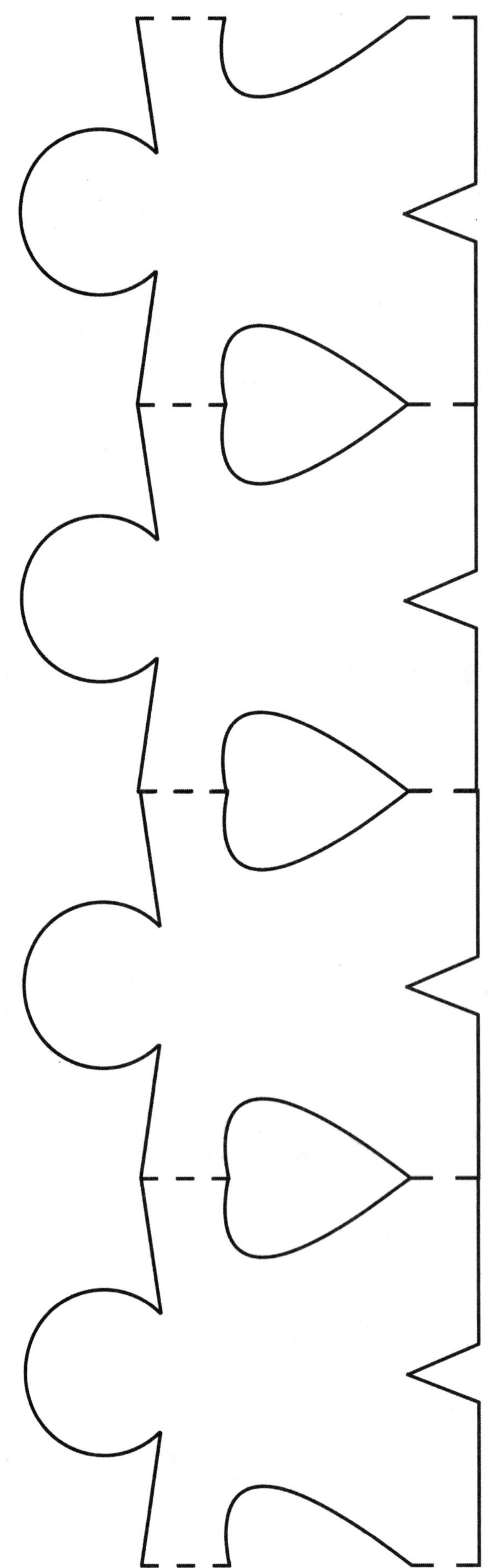